Terry Gould

IS YOUR EYES ON TRACK?

Improving provision and outcomes for the children in your setting

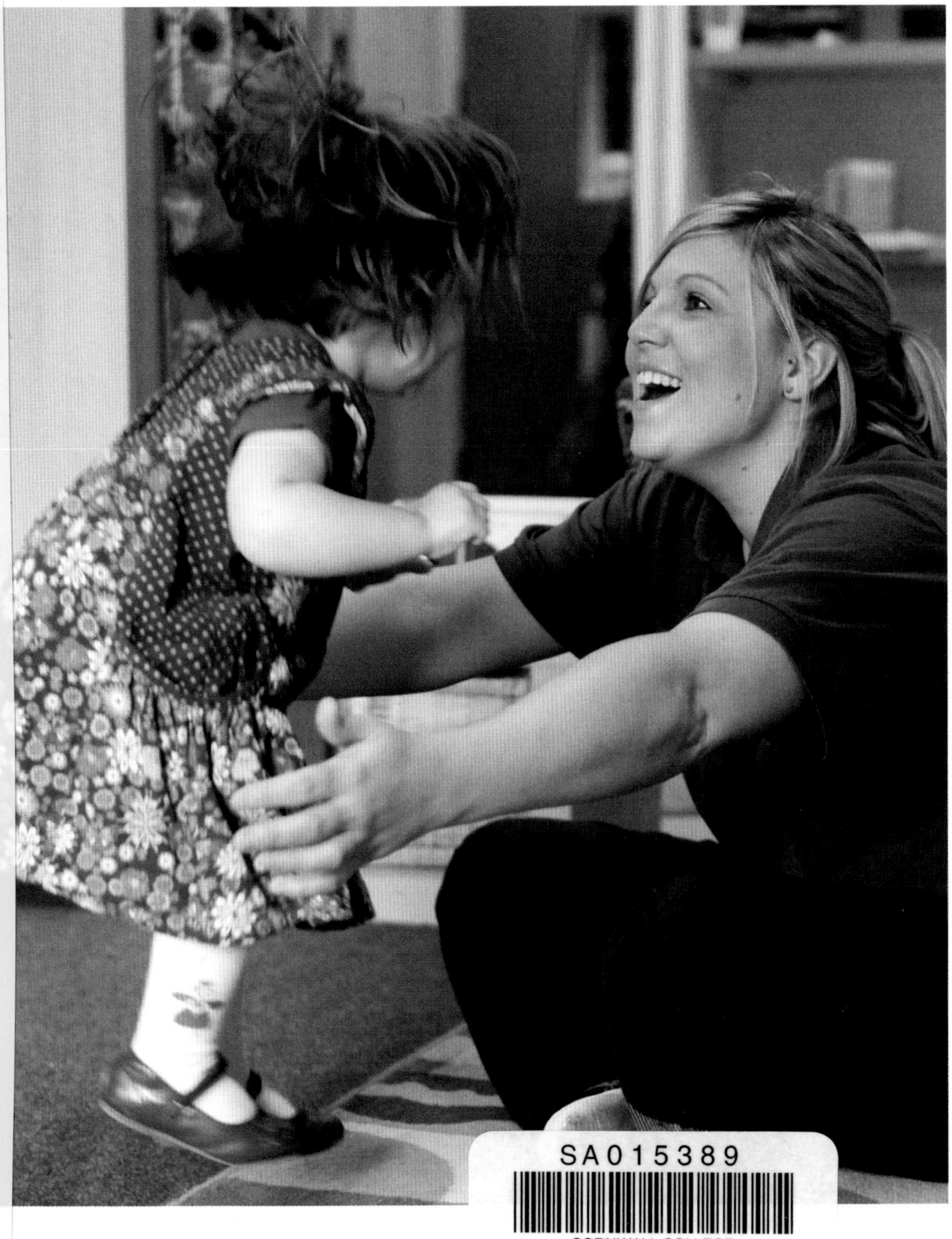

Published 2012 by Featherstone Education
Bloomsbury Publishing Plc
50 Bedford Square, London, WC1B 3DP
www.bloomsbury.com

ISBN 978-1-4081-6-3979

A CIP record for this publication is available from the British Library.

Printed in Great Britain by Latimer Trend & Company Ltd

10 9 8 7 6 5 4 3 2 1

This book is produced using paper that is made from wood grown in managed, sustainable forests. It is natural, renewable and recyclable. The logging and manufacturing processes conform to the environmental regulations of the country of origin.

To see our full range of titles visit www.bloomsbury.com

Acknowledgements
Grateful thanks from the author and publishing team are extended to the children and settings who have allowed their images to be used in this book. We hope that you will enjoy seeing yourself in print!

Acorn Childcare Ltd
Bertram Nursery Group
COSY Ltd
Kids Unlimited Group
Little Hulton SSCC
St Margaret Ward RC Primary School

Contents

Introduction ... 4

Chapter 1
Self-evaluation starts with celebration ... 6

Chapter 2
Outcomes for children ... 16

Chapter 3
The quality of the provision ... 32

Chapter 4
Effective leadership and management ... 36

Chapter 5
Overall effectiveness ... 40

Chapter 6
Good practice audits ... 43

Bibliography and further reading ... 64

Introduction

> The very best providers use their evaluations to strengthen and build on the most effective practice and to remedy any weaknesses they find in areas that are not as good.
>
> **Ofsted (2011)**

- **What is self-evaluation?**
- **Why is self-evaluation important?**
- **What should the process of self-evaluation include?**

These are some of the key questions to be explored by this book.

Practitioners in good Early Years settings have always carried out self-evaluation on all aspects of their provision and practice. Now that there is the freedom to undertake self-evaluation in a setting's own preferred way, there is for some a need for direction in how to do this, which is both objective and systematic. It is important that self-evaluation is effectively undertaken because it really does help to drive improvement of the overall quality of provision and outcomes for children. Most adults working with children aged 0–5 years undertake self-evaluation at some level. The key question is how well do they undertake this and how well does it then support a vision of the improvements to be made?

Children, as well as practitioners, can be involved in the self-evaluation process. They can, and should be, supported to self-evaluate at an appropriate level, by practitioners who should encourage them to reflect on what is provided for them. Children should be encouraged to reflect on things in ways that help them to consider what could be done to improve or make things better for them to learn and develop. Key provocative/challenging questions should be used by adults with children.

Parents should, wherever possible, be included in the self-evaluation process too on a scale with which they feel comfortable. An example is for them to give periodic feedback to the setting via their child's key person, on what they feel works well and what could be changed for the benefit of their child.

There is, however, one very important aspect of self-evaluation to bear in mind throughout the process:

> high quality and effective self-evaluation makes the important more easily measurable rather than making the easily measurable more important.
>
> **Gould, T. (2009)**

Keeping hold of this idea is one of the most important things within the process.

Terry Gould

Chapter 1
Self-evaluation starts with celebration

> Inspections focus on how well individual children benefit from their early years experience............... by observing how well they help all children to make effective progress, especially those whose needs or circumstances require particularly perceptive intervention and/or additional support.
>
> **Ofsted (July 2012)**

The starting point for all effective self-evaluation is to identify **what is already good**. This is one key element that is all too easy to overlook in the race to improve. To become more effective providers, all practitioners in an EYFS setting need to focus as a team on getting the basics right in every aspect, and in every area of their practice and provision. Self-evaluation should be undertaken by whole teams and not looked upon as simply another task for leadership and management. If all staff work together to reflect on their practice, and their setting's overall provision, it will enable a shared understanding to be established around their roles, responsibilities and accountability.

The main purpose of self-evaluation is to raise standards relating to care, learning and teaching, remembering the principle that **education and care are inseparable**. The self-evaluation process is all about building capacity for improvement, including the creation of a vision where the setting aims to improve within a specific time scale. Whichever aspect of self-evaluation is taking place, it must be in the context that (whilst it needs to identify and recognise growth points) it should start with **celebrating** the things that are already good.

Many years of experience of leading on improvements in schools and other settings has shown me that there is a need to build the capacity of the management team and the rest of the staff in order to be able to move practice and provision forward. This means having people in post with the right developed skills and vision to make the necessary changes and this includes having the following:

- **A clear and *shared vision*: the senior management team need to involve and lead the whole team in developing a vision that is understood and shared by everyone.**

- ***Strong, supportive* but challenging leadership:** there is a fine balance between challenging and undermining. Where the challenges require hard messages, these can be delivered in ways that inspire rather than undermine goodwill and confidence. An effective leader is able to bring the team with him/her on the improvement journey. Any training or coaching required to further develop capacity needs to be identified and then put into place.

- **Establishing a climate of trust within a culture of team work:** challenging leadership needs to be within an appropriate climate that helps all staff to feel trusted and valued, with a sense of belonging to a team that is on the way to being successful. Staff need to feel that they have a leader who is fair, competent and on whom they can rely. To achieve this, time needs to be invested to clarify roles within the team and to listen to the views and ideas of the team.

- **Clarity of roles and ownership of the move forward towards improvement:** where roles are clear and staff know who is to take responsibility for doing what, and where management listen to staff ideas and views, and then respond, there is a stronger sense of ownership which helps to motivate the team.

- **Reviewing and measuring progress made through a strong focus on performance management:** there is need for a clear and detailed action plan that is specific enough to allow periodic reviews of progress to take place, and to know if the improvement programme is on track or not.

NB There may well be a need for external advice, input, coaching or training to support these objectives and this should be identified and arranged from the start of the process.

Having a clear vision cannot be underestimated and it is important that, before beginning the journey of improvement towards outstanding, a team considers the steps that this will involve and how these can best be approached, so as to maximise progress within a specific time scale.

Keller and Price (2011) identify a useful five-stage process for developing capabilities beyond current performance:

- **Aspire – Where do we want to go?**
- **Assess – How ready are we to go there?**
- **Architect – What do we need to get there?**
- **Act – How do we manage the journey?**
- **Advance – How do we keep moving forward?**

I would advise schools/settings to add a further overarching stage to these five stages:

- **Aware – How can we ensure there is no slippage in our action plans?**

Using these six stages will help any school/setting to make those first steps and then keep on track towards the agreed targets for improvement. This will involve identifying where practice is already going well. Celebrating good practice should always be the starting point, remembering that 'self-evaluation starts with celebration' by identifying existing good practice. This is important for two main reasons:

- **It enables existing good practice to be maintained as part of the action plan.**
- **It supports staff morale both within the development of a climate of trust and a culture of team work.**

Having identified all of this, a key question often asked is, where should we, as a team, begin to self-evaluate our EYFS provision?

This is likely to vary from school/setting to school/setting and depends on where each is currently up to in their ongoing development. The need for self-evaluation to start within specific areas can come from a variety of triggers, such as:

- **a recent Ofsted inspection that has highlighted areas for development**
- **a local authority or independent adviser who has undertaken some detailed observations and fed these back**
- **data trends which are significantly below national expectations**
- **the management team wanting to review aspects of practice for a specific reason (for example, following a national revision of the EYFS Framework, feedback from parents, observations by the senior management team and/or governing body, or other relevant visitors).**

Wherever self-evaluation begins, it must cover two key areas:

1. **meeting the statutory requirements**
2. **ensuring the provision of good practice**

and should bear in mind the four key or main judgement areas for all EYFS Ofsted inspections, which are:

- **outcomes for children**
- **the quality of provision**
- **the effectiveness of leadership and management**
- **overall effectiveness – how well the setting/school meets the needs of all children.**

Within the statutory requirements, the following three key sections need to be focused on for self-evaluation:

- **learning and development requirements**
- **assessment requirements**
- **safeguarding and welfare requirements.**

These three key sections are underpinned by good practice, which should be shaped by the four guiding principles of Statutory Framework, DfE, 2012:

* **Every child is unique, is constantly learning and can be resilient, capable, confident and self-assured.**
* **Children learn to be strong and independent through positive relationships.**
* **Children learn and develop well in enabling environments, in which their experiences respond to their individual needs and there is a strong partnership between practitioners and parents/carers.**
* **Children develop and learn in different ways and at different rates.**

The previous four principles are supported by practice that delivers:

- **quality and consistency** in all schools/settings, so that every child makes good progress and no child gets left behind
- **a secure foundation** through learning and development opportunities, planned around the needs and interests of each individual child and are assessed and reviewed regularly
- **partnership working** between practitioners and parents/carers
- **equality of opportunity** and anti-discriminatory practice, ensuring that every child is included and supported.
  (Statutory Framework, DfE, 2012)

Within the good practice requirements five key areas that are recommended for focus on are:

1. Observation, assessment and planning

2. Quality learning environments (indoors and outdoors)

3. An effective routine

4. The quality of learning and teaching

5. Organised and effective roles of practitioners

1 Observation, assessment and planning

- Do all staff reflect on daily observations with a focus on children's interests, and value contributions from parents/carers so as to plan the next steps in children's learning?
- Does the provision ensure that there are times and places for children to meet their individual needs and interests, which allow for both planned and spontaneous opportunities?
- Is there an appropriate balance of child-initiated and adult-led/planned activities that enable all children at whatever stage of development to participate and succeed?
- Is appropriate value placed on children's own ideas and interests?
- Are individual children's learning and development needs valued and supported by practitioners?
- Do practitioners record and then use significant observations of child-initiated activities to identify the learning taking place and to support the assessment, recording and planning process?
- Are individual learning and development records maintained for each child which take on board evidence from child-initiated and adult-led activities and for which parental contributions are encouraged, and value placed on these?
- Are individual records regularly shared with parents, and their comments recorded and taken on board?

2 Quality learning environments (indoors and outdoors)

> Education must come to be recognised as the product of a set of complex interactions, many of which can be realised only when the environment is a fully participating element.
>
> **Malguzzi (2000)**

> Children should have access to high-quality early years provision in order to make the most of their talents and abilities.
>
> **Ofsted (July 2012)**

- **Are rooms clearly defined into interest or workshop type areas that are stage appropriate?**
- **Do room spaces and furniture allow all individuals and groups of children to access and use all the areas in free-play activity?**
- **Is all furniture and flooring fit for purpose and stage appropriate, for example, cosy and comfortable, and of the right height and size?**
- **Are children able to freely access the outdoor space/s every day for substantial periods of sustained involvement?**
- **Is provision made for children to freely access outdoor space/s in all weathers, and is there sufficient shade and shelter made available?**
- **Do the outdoor play spaces offer a variety of surfaces for children to explore, for example, grass, hard surfacing, bark and soft surfacing?**
- **Are toys and other learning resources clean and safe, and maintained in good condition?**
- **Are all toys and other learning resources attractive, interesting and appropriate for the stage of development of the children using them?**
- **In the indoor environment, is there a stage appropriate balance between the use of floor space and table tops for activities?**
- **Are the resources at the height of the children, easily accessible and well labelled using words and pictures with some, as appropriate, in dual languages?**
- **Is there a wide range of open-ended and natural resources, for example, corks, pinecones, straws and shells?**
- **Are the resources/materials for indoor and outdoor use varied, inclusive, stimulating, stage appropriate and supportive of all seven areas of learning and development, both prime and specific?**
- **Do resources and materials appropriately reflect the children's changing needs and interests, and the local/wider community, and do visual images and resources reflect the children's home life and the communities of the children in the setting?**
- **How effectively and appropriately do practitioners promote the use of resources that reflect a range and variety of cultures, ethnic groups, communities, gender roles and disabilities, for example, do adults promote diversity in positive ways and use stage appropriate visual images and play resources?**
- **Are there interactive and other displays at the children's height/level that are easily accessible to them and are informative, stimulating and supportive of further learning, and which value the things that children create, make and do?**

3 An effective routine

An effective routine for the day that supports an appropriate balance between adult-led and child-initiated learning

- Are routines consistent and supported by a visual timetable that helps children to understand and recognise the pattern of the day?
- Do practitioners understand and recognise the importance of a routine that allows for flexibility, including showing children how to initiate and sustain their involvement in their own play?
- Where appropriate, does the routine of the day allow opportunities for practitioners to provide support to extend and develop children's learning and development through their self-initiated play?
- How well do adults communicate their intentions to children before and during care routines, and are babies always held by their key person (except on rare, unavoidable occasions) whilst feeding them from a bottle?
- Are care routines flexible enough to allow practitioners to follow the individual needs of children (for example, allowing them to sleep and wake in their own time)?
- Do practitioners very rarely expect children to wait until all others are finished or ready, for example, going outdoors, at meal times, in circle/group time activities?
- Do practitioners give appropriate advance warning for children to bring their play to a close, for example, at lunch time and before group/circle time?
- Do practitioners and children work together to tidy away resources and do they find ways to make tidy-up time fun?
- Do children know where the resources are located and are they supported appropriately to encourage them to return these after use and/or at the end of the session?

The quality of learning and teaching

Playing and exploring – engagement

Do practitioners effectively help children to:

- **find out and explore?**
- **play with what they know?**
- **be willing to 'have a go'?**

Active learning – motivation

Do practitioners effectively help children to:

- **be involved and concentrate?**
- **keep trying?**
- **enjoy achieving what they set out to do?**

Creating and thinking critically – thinking

Do practitioners effectively help children to:

- **have their own ideas?**
- **make links?**
- **choose ways to do things?**

(as identified in Development Matters, 2012, pages 6–8)
As well as:

Sustained involvement – perseverance

Do practitioners effectively help children to:

- **have intrinsic enjoyment?**
- **be stimulated by the activity?**
- **be in control of their own learning?**

Factors of the child's persona

Do practitioners effectively help children to develop their:

- **self-confidence?**
- **independence and self-help skills?**
- **language and communication skills?**
- **social skills?**

5 Organised and effective roles of practitioners

* Do all practitioners readily respond to children's attempts to communicate and show a genuine interest when interacting with them?
* Are children encouraged by the strategies of practitioners to take the lead in conversations?
* Do adults, as much as possible, ask open-ended questions and make comments to encourage conversation, and do they give sufficient time for children to respond to any question posed to them by adults?
* Are the moods and feelings of children always acknowledged and considered by practitioners?
* Are children's individual ideas and efforts always fully responded to, encouraged and valued by explicit positive comments and other suitable responses?
* Are all practitioners sensitive to the impact of children's individual well-being on their learning and development, for example, home circumstances or physical/medical needs?
* Do all practitioners handle unwanted behaviours in consistent ways, in line with the setting's behaviour policy, which allow children to reflect on their behaviour, explain problems and suggest solutions?
* Does the key person, or the regular support assistant for children with SEN or additional medical/physical needs, always provide the majority of the personal care throughout the day for each child?
* How well do all adults recognise and make responses that value children's self-initiated play?
* How effectively and regularly are parents/carers kept informed of their child's daily routine and their achievements, and is there high importance placed on regular meetings with parents/carers to keep them updated about their child's progress?

- How well do practitioners ensure that all arrivals and departures are warm, happy, relaxed and personal?
- Are children's feelings about separation verbalised and respected in stage appropriate ways, with comforters always accessible, for example, babies are comforted and reassured until they are calmer?
- Are transitions made as smooth as possible through the use of effective strategies with parents/carers, the key person and the child, and other agencies involved with planning arrangements for the move from one stage to the next?
- Is there a pleasant and relaxed atmosphere created for children and staff through an ethos of team working, supported by the management?

An effective focus on these areas will lead to improved outcomes for all children, which takes us nicely into the next chapter, entitled *Outcomes for children.*

Chapter 2
Outcomes for children

How well the early years provision meets the needs of the range of children who attend and is reflected in their achievements

> Inspectors will assess "the extent to which children enjoy their learning and achieve well; feel safe; learn to lead healthy lifestyles; make a positive contribution; and develop their skills for the future".
>
> **Ofsted (2012)**

As identified earlier, the main purpose of self-evaluation is to improve standards of provision and, as a result, outcomes for children. When inspectors make their visit to your school/setting, they will take into account the evidence you have gathered and the judgements you have made as part of your self-evaluation. They will then observe the practice of the staff, the provision indoors and outdoors, and the responses of the children to the learning opportunities offered. They will also look at written records, talk with children, staff and parents, and through this make judgements around the five aspects of Every Child Matters, including outcomes for children and what it is like for a child attending your setting.

The inspection in the area of 'Outcomes for Children' continues focus on the five outcomes of Every Child Matters, and their starting points from first attending the setting. Hence, whenever children begin at your setting, over the first 6–8 week period of their attendance, you should use observational judgements to create a baseline of what they know and can do. This will then allow you to plan to meet their needs and be able to demonstrate the progress the children have made/are making as they continue to attend. The evidence that settings can provide, as part of their self-evaluation, is often all around and yet, on occasions, many settings struggle to think what they can use to really show the quality of what they provide and how they act. The breadth and variety of some of the types of evidence that can be used is listed over the next few pages. Using this, you should have much less difficulty in identifying as a team what you do well and where you could improve further, and thus raise the quality of your self-evaluation and progress.

Remember that as part of the self-evaluation process, it is important to gather evidence of the things you do to improve/change the provision, such as:

- **photographic evidence**
- **written documentation**
- **training records.**

Also, where possible, it is important to document the impact these have on improved outcomes for the children.

The EYFS revised Framework guidance (2012) advocates children learning through play and exploration, and it is important for you to self-evaluate whether your children have a balanced diet of play. To undertake this, children's play can be broken down into three main areas, although there are many activities in which these overlap. The whole team needs to reflect on whether the children are able to access a balance of the three areas at a stage appropriate level and how you enable this to happen over the weeks/year.

The three main areas I have identified are:

- **Creative/messy play: in this type of play, children engage in making things, including creating models, paintings, baking and making music, as well as exploring and experimenting with natural materials such as water, sand, dough and clay.**
- **Imaginative/copycat play: in this type of play, children engage in playing out their experiences, including copying what they have seen adults doing. They begin to imaginatively use one object to represent another, playing by taking on different roles that they feel they know and understand.**
- **Active/physical play: in this type of play, children move around using their physical skills, including running, climbing, throwing, jumping, hopping, kicking, rolling, crawling and dancing.**

Children will naturally engage in child-initiated play, but there are many times when adults can suggest, lead or model some ideas to take this forward.

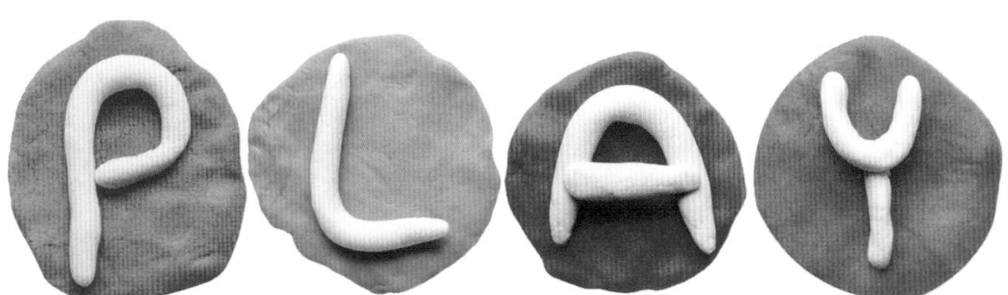

The five outcomes from Every Child Matters

> An evaluation of the provision for children's learning and development is determined by the knowledge, understanding, skills and attitudes they are helped to acquire, and their progress towards the Early Learning Goals, during their time at the setting. Inspectors should draw evidence from across provision for all five Every Child Matters outcomes.
>
> **Ofsted Guidance for Inspectors (April 2012)**

1 A Focus on enjoying and achieving

When inspectors observe children at play and actively engaged in their learning, they will be looking to find evidence that children enjoy attending the setting and that they are making good progress in their learning and development. They will want to see whether practitioners interact sensitively with the children and are providing an appropriate range of experiences through which children will develop their knowledge, skills, ideas, thinking, understanding and interests. They will seek to establish if all practitioners demonstrate that they acknowledge children as active learners and provide the right kind of experiences for them to learn through active engagement appropriate to their stage of development.

They will listen to how practitioners interact with children, including their use of open-ended questioning, non-verbal communication and how they respond to what children say and do. Remember the characteristics of effective learning include creating and thinking (Development Matters, Early Education, 2012).

Inspectors will expect to see some written planning and they will check whether there are clear purposes identified, appropriate differentiation is in place and how observations are used to plan the next steps in children's learning and development. In line with this, it is important that any records of children's achievement are kept up to date and are based on both evidence for adult-planned/led activities and also for child-initiated play, and exploration indoors and outdoors.

Consider focusing on the following and then using evidence in your self-evaluations:

- **deployment of staff**
- **organisation of space, indoors and outdoors**
- **staff training/knowledge on Development Matters/Early Learning Goals (ELGs)**
- **the quality, range and diversity of resources provided**
- **the nature of the access to resources for all children**
- **initiatives/activity plans, for example, '3 A Day Stories'**
- **quality and range of ICT provision**
- **children's progress meetings**
- **planning records, including continuous planning and adult-led planning links to the revised EYFS Development Matters/ELGs in all seven areas of learning 'Prime and Specific'**
- **identification and response to individual learning styles by the differentiation of play and learning**

- mission statement: aims and objectives
- parent/carer pack/handbook and information on the nature of the partnership with parents/carers, plus work undertaken with parents/carers to identify their child's likes and dislikes, and general needs
- transition practice
- diaries/general records
- routines and procedures of the day/week
- opportunities for sharing stories, songs, rhymes and games with children
- the range of opportunities for supporting and encouraging speaking and listening skills
- the nature of the opportunities for children to explore and discover through sensory play and activities
- opportunities provided for mark making/writing/drawing in child-initiated and adult-supported play and activities

- the quality of observations, assessment and record-keeping, as well as children's profile records/learning journeys and any other children's developmental records
- support and encouragement provided to children for developing positive attitudes to learning
- the staff development and training programme provided and how this has impacted on outcomes for children
- the overall quality of accessible play and learning opportunities indoors and outdoors
- staff awareness and understanding of children's individual needs and interests
- access to, and use of, alternative/additional communication methods/systems, for example, signing, visual timetable or PECs.

Also consider your policies and records that can relate to children enjoying and achieving, such as your:

- setting's operational/development plan
- SEN policy and working with regard to the current SEN code of practice and DDA requirements
- behaviour management policy and the named behaviour management lead and their experience/expertise
- evidence of activities and opportunities to develop children's emotional, physical, social and intellectual capabilities, for example, SEAL
- observational-based summaries in children's learning journeys (completed every 6–8 weeks)
- transition policy
- inclusion policy
- managers'/leaders' weekly monitoring notebook
- EYFSP records (children attending at reception age stage)
- policy on learning and teaching
- parents' recorded comments.

Additional ideas that can also be considered include:

- **type/nature of displays: images are good here with annotated notes**
- **effective transition evidence/feedback**
- **videos of children learning through play and exploration at the setting, and other still photographic evidence**
- **appropriate balance of adult-led and child-initiated learning opportunities**
- **home/school support for speaking and listening, for example, Through Firm Foundations and/or PEPL.**

2 A Focus on staying safe

Keeping children safe is a wide reaching/all-encompassing concept, and covers both physical and emotional aspects. Inspectors will want to see that the environment that your setting is offering is bright, clean and well maintained so that it is both physically and emotionally comfortable for the children who attend. This means that there is a consistency of quality across all the rooms and areas within the setting. It is no use having a superb baby room which is then let down by a poor pre-school room, or a superb nursery class which is then let down by a poor reception class!

As inspectors will rightly focus on the emotional aspects of staying safe as well as the physical aspects, then it makes sense that you self-evaluate and gather evidence for both of these. Some aspects of provision cover both elements, such as there being sufficient space for children to move around and having a designated area for rest/sleep. Inspectors will make notes on a range of practices, including whether children are encouraged to use the toilets independently and whether the toilets and the nappy-changing areas demonstrate due regard for the privacy of the child. Having no doors on the toilets would not demonstrate this, nor would a nappy-changing area on full view. They will also check whether fresh bedding is provided when children require a rest/sleep and how children are encouraged to learn about health and safety issues in appropriate ways, and to learn why these are important.

Records of fire drills will be checked as well as annual appliance inspections, and the general management of the provision. A radiator not working in the bathroom on a cold day would come under general management issues for keeping safe as would no warm water from taps for hand washing – and I have known both of these to become a limiting factor in the overall inspection outcome! This is why it must be a team effort and every practitioner must keep on top of things that are required to be maintained by bringing any issues to the management's attention as soon as these are noted.

There are new requirements in the revised EYFS Framework (DfE, 2012) for all staff to be trained in responding to concerns around safeguarding/welfare. Inspectors will want to know that this has been taken on board, with a suitable designated person to advise and support staff in this area.

Consider focusing on the following and then using evidence in your self-evaluations from:

- the ways you have organised and used the space
- information/data storage, for example, IEPs
- kitchen facilities, for example, hygiene or healthy meals inspection reports
- quality of resources and equipment, including maintenance/safety checks
- safe access to resources for children, for example, not too much in boxes and stored at a child's height
- activity plans
- any risk assessments undertaken
- procedures for care, repair and replacement of toys/resources
- record of visitors to the setting
- CRB records – all staff and regular visitors
- secure and safe nature of the outdoor area

- collection of children procedures
- missing child procedures
- opportunities for children's decision making to take place
- how children are supported to learn about rules, boundaries and keeping safe
- links to developmental matters for PSE, Physical Development and Understanding of the World, for example, road safety, use of tools and equipment, healthy practices – sleep, healthy eating, exercise, visits from or to the nurse, the doctor, the dentist and personal safety awareness
- accessibility of play and learning opportunities
- staff awareness of children's individual needs
- risk assessment for children with identified needs, for example, medical or behavioural
- staff training in safe moving and handling
- moving and handling assessments carried out for identified children.

Also consider your policies and records relating to children staying safe, such as:

- health and safety policy
- children's individual records
- accident records
- changes to premises documentation
- fire safety policy
- fire drill record
- safeguarding/child protection policy
- allegations against staff policy
- public liability certificate
- named child protection officer
- named first aiders
- behaviour policy/named behaviour management lead
- SEN policy and named SENCO
- policy for working with regard to SEN code of practice and DDA
- medication and emergency treatment consent
- first aid boxes.

Additional ideas to consider:

* locks on cupboards containing cleaning materials etc.
* front door/gates security
* emergency password in the event of a major incident
* suitable outdoor clothing for trips out or in an outdoor area.

3 A Focus on keeping healthy

Settings that achieve well within this outcome are kept clean and hygienic. The resources and equipment are appropriately well maintained and cared for on an ongoing regular basis. Only medicines authorised by parents are given and their provision is logged, dated and signed. Children receive appropriate first aid that is recorded and countersigned by their parents/carers. On a daily basis, children are offered a wide range of fresh fruit and vegetables, and are able to access drinking water freely.

The provision of the setting ensures that children have opportunities throughout the day to engage in activities which support small and large physical skills, and hand–eye co-ordination skills, both indoors and outdoors, including those for vigorous exercise. Before eating meals or snacks, children wash their hands and are reminded /supported by practitioners to do so, including by using signs and audio message systems.

Keeping healthy really matters for young children in the EYFS. The implications of eating a healthy diet and engaging with appropriate levels of physical exercise are important for the child's well-being both now and in the future. Children who are healthy and alert are more able and ready to learn and their attendance is often better. They are stronger and happier in their lives as a result of recognition by practitioners and parents that care and education are inseparable elements.

Consider focusing on the following and then using evidence in your self-evaluations form:

- **activity plans for physical development**
- **indoor/outdoor plans for continuous provision, showing opportunities/ resources for physical activities and skills**
- **menus: snacks and lunch**
- **displays on being healthy, for example, healthy eating/washing hands**
- **parents' notice boards**
- **everyday routines to promote safety and hygiene**
- **access to drinks and water**
- **rest times**
- **the way a setting recognises and supports individual preferences and needs, for example, dietary requirements**
- **links to Developmental Matters for Personal, Social and Emotional Development, Physical Development and Knowledge of the World, for example, daily provision for indoor and outdoor activities, ways of promoting self-esteem and emotional well-being, and the setting's philosophy for positive attitudes to being healthy**
- **the way dietary items are included to meet individual needs i.e. cultural, special, medical and allergies**
- **access and use of any specialist equipment for feeding, if any**
- **ongoing information and liaison with parents and other professionals**
- **information sharing relating to individual children's care and medical needs with all staff.**

Also consider your policies and records relating to children keeping healthy, such as:

- health and safety policy
- parent partnership links relating to this area
- record of medicines administered to children
- no smoking signs and policy
- how children are encouraged to be independent
- healthy eating policy
- sickness policy
- key person policy/practice
- accident signed record book/files
- notifiable diseases record (as defined by the Health Protection Agency)
- first aid certificates: paediatric/names of designated first aiders and first aid kits
- food hygiene and other certificates, such as those in nutrition and environmental health
- any risk assessments completed.

Further ideas to consider as evidence include:

- displays, for example, on washing hands
- good access to an attached and well-developed outdoor area with designated space for running and ball play etc.
- trips taken to the park etc. – how often is to be stated
- how children are encouraged to talk with staff about the importance of being active
- self-service at lunch times – children are able to make their own healthy choices, with appropriately sized portions
- weekly dance class in the setting (if any)
- swimming once a week from the setting (if any)
- health visitor coming in to talk with the children, bringing in interesting/exciting artefacts etc.
- teeth-brushing programme (if any)
- Top Start type physical development programmes, planning to cover four areas of basic motor skills (if any)
- active fun days with things like obstacle courses, knock-over bottles and hook-a-duck etc.

A Focus on making a positive contribution

Children within this outcome should be supported to engage in activities that enable them to express their developing awareness of their own cultures and beliefs. The resources that are provided must be free from gender or stereotype bias, and must promote positive images of society.

Practitioners in the setting will need to work together and, with other professionals, set stage-appropriate challenges for children to learn at their own level of development and understanding. They will need to plan within this for children's individual needs and interests. This will likely involve visits out to local places of interest as well as visits in from members of the local community. A key person system will be effectively in place and practitioners will model appropriate behaviour and show genuine respect for each other and the children. Children's skills in conflict resolution will be supported by adults and this will be enhanced by an effective behaviour management policy that is consistently applied by all the staff team.

The ethos of the setting will promote adults to encourage children to be actively involved in their own learning. Adults and children should be having fun sharing and exploring new concepts and developing ideas. Care and education will be seen as inseparable and care routines will be undertaken wherever possible by the child's key person.

Consider focusing on the following and then using evidence in your self-evaluations form:

- **effective partnership with parents**
- **parents' handbook**
- **parents' information sessions/visits**
- **transition procedures**
- **ground rules/golden rules**
- **children engaging in decision making, supporting groups/communities, e.g. fund raising**
- **opportunities for children to enjoy time with trusted and familiar others**
- **links to PSE Development Matters/ELGs**
- **opportunities for children to develop positive images, self-confidence and self-esteem, independent learning skills, sense of community and problem-solving skills**
- **links with outside agencies, e.g. health, police and fire**
- **availability and range of resources that reflect diversity, e.g. disability, religion and culture**
- **information presented in different formats, e.g. signs, pictures to support children's understanding, and ability to engage in decision making, requests and routines.**

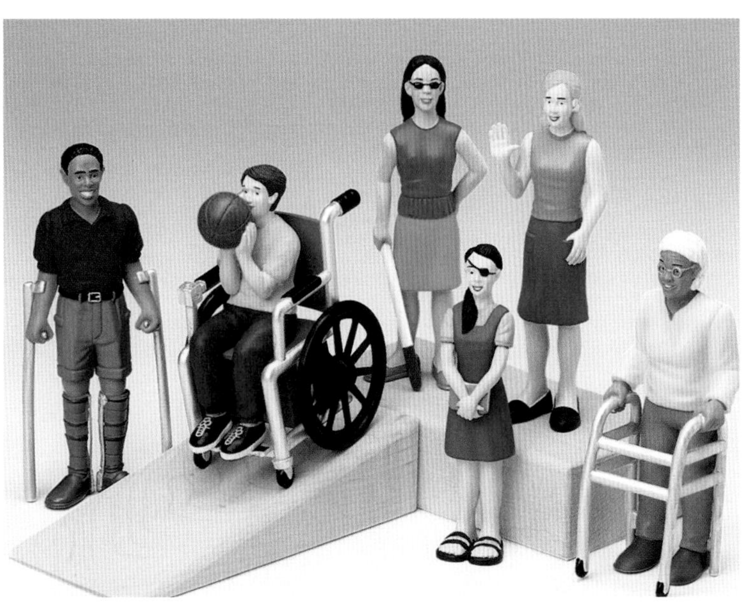

Also consider your policies and records relating to children making a positive contribution, such as:

- operational plan
- behaviour policy and its consistent use – positive behaviour strategies agreed with parents and used consistently
- SEN policy – working with regard to SEN code of practice and DDA
- evidence of activities and opportunities to develop children's emotional, physical, social and intellectual capabilities
- children's learning journeys/development files and observational-based summaries/child voice sheets (completed every 6–8 weeks)
- planning documentation
- notes from advisory teacher/consultancy support visits
- inclusion policy and equal opportunities policy
- accurate and updated records of children's/ parents' names, addresses, dates of births and contact telephone numbers
- complaints policy and procedures
- time when practitioners talk about 'When I grow up, I want to be...'

5 A Focus on developing skills for the fututre

Within this outcome, the skills that children develop as communicators, problem solvers and thinkers in the EYFS will be critical in ensuring that what they learn is useful and transferable as they move through their schooling and into the workplace and adulthood. To enable this to happen, there will be a robust focus on recruiting and retaining an experienced and committed team of practitioners. They will all have up-to-date CRB checks in place and suitable ongoing training in the revised EYFS, as well as training to support the safeguarding of children.

Policies and procedures in settings with good provision will be consistently followed by all staff to ensure children's welfare, and practitioners will be regularly involved in reviewing such policies. ICT experiences and skills are diverse and stage appropriate. They will be provided with an understanding that ICT will likely have an importance in all future life and work situations for the children.

Practitioners in a setting with good practice will reflect on the quality of experiences and outcomes every day, for every child, understanding the concept that the whole day matters. Management will provide purposeful and effective leadership that supports all the team, having a sound grasp of the strengths and weaknesses of the setting with all staff recognising their shared responsibility for the effective running of the setting.

Consider focusing on the following and then using evidence in your self-evaluations form:

- **planning records**
- **children's developmental records**
- **learning environments (indoors and outdoors)**
- **quality and range of ICT provision**
- **partnership with parents**
- **routines**
- **key person system**
- **differentiation for individual children to meet their needs and interests**
- **SENCo role and action plans**
- **quality and range of resources and equipment**
- **behaviour policy**
- **effectiveness of support for language and communication**
- **links to Understanding of the World, Development Matters/ELGs.**

Also consider your policies and records relating to children developing skills for the future, such as:

- prospectus/setting brochure
- displays including photographic evidence
- continuous provision planning for indoors and outdoors
- partnership with parents – children's progress meetings
- learning and teaching policy
- staff training and development plans and records
- manager's monitoring notebook
- staff observations of children
- EYFSP records (only children attending at reception-age stage).

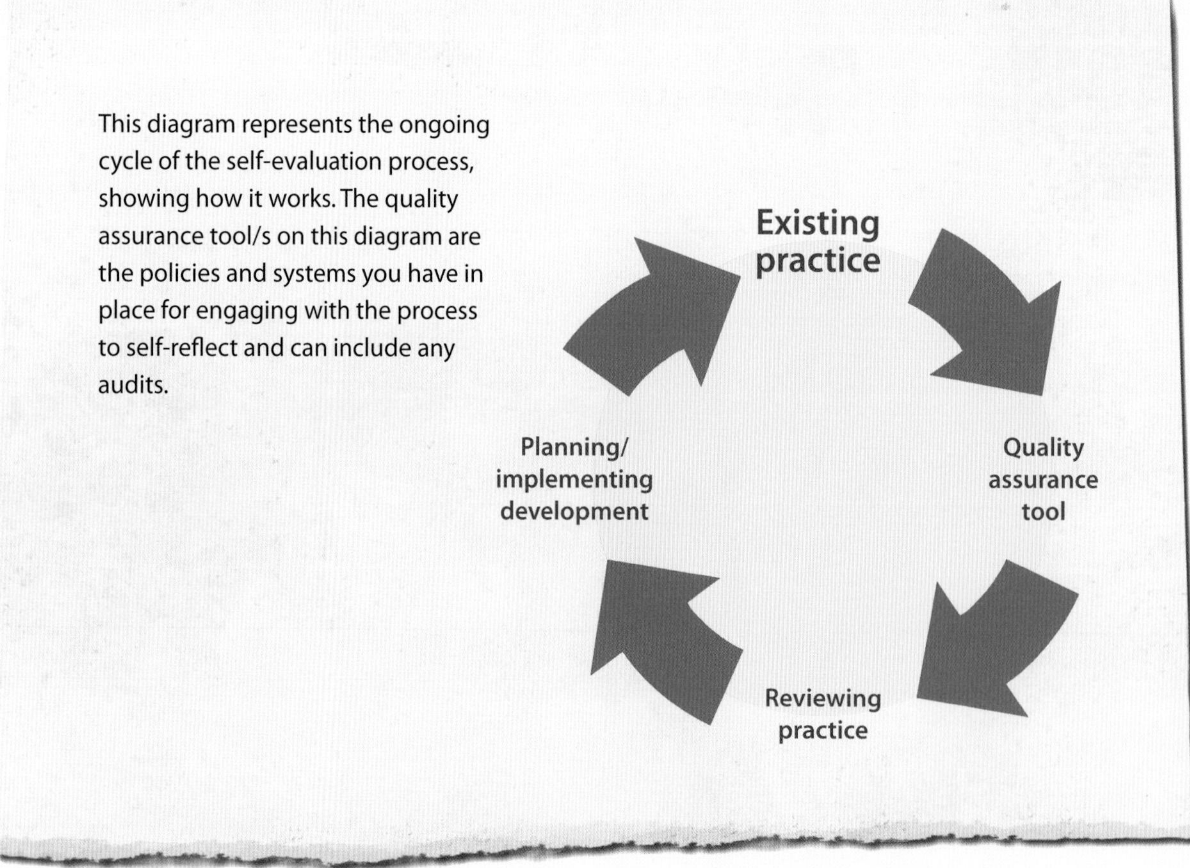

This diagram represents the ongoing cycle of the self-evaluation process, showing how it works. The quality assurance tool/s on this diagram are the policies and systems you have in place for engaging with the process to self-reflect and can include any audits.

More reflective questions to discuss as a team are listed below and these reflect some of the questions inspectors may ask:

- How well do the children attending your setting achieve and how can you demonstrate this in each Prime Area: Communication and Language, Physical, Personal, Social and Emotional, and in each Specific Area: Literacy, Mathematics, Understanding the World, and Expressive Arts and Design?
- Are all staff fully involved in setting up and reviewing school/setting policies?
- How often and how well do you actively take up and respond to the views of parents/carers?
- Do you have continuous indoor/outdoor provision in place throughout the day and, if not, how do you ensure that children are able to fully access their entitlement to quality outdoor learning opportunities?
- How do you ensure that parents are kept well informed and up to date on their children's progress and what is provided for them to learn?
- Are quality observations being undertaken and then used to plan for the next steps in children's learning?
- Does the indoor and the outdoor environment offer an appropriately high level of accessible learning opportunities that are stage appropriate across all seven areas of learning and development?
- Is the planning that you complete effective for all children and does it allow for an appropriate balance between child-initiated and adult-led learning?
- Are the premises clean, well organised and well lit?
- Is ICT offered in meaningful ways that support and enhance learning opportunities and outcomes?
- How do you ensure that transition is as smooth/seamless as possible for all groups of children and at all stages?
- How does your policy and practice ensure all children are supported to be safe and healthy?
- Are all children able to access a balance of quality play at a stage-appropriate level, both indoors and outdoors?

Outcomes for children very much depend upon the quality of the resources and experiences that are provided for them by the school/setting. This is done through a stimulating, engaging, learning environment, indoors and outdoors, with a team of practitioners who are knowledgeable, experienced and committed to the children. These are key aspects of the quality of effective provision that enables children to maximise their potential.

Chapter 3
The quality of the provision

Significantly including the contribution of the early years provision to children's well-being

> *Children develop in the context of the enabling environment around them, and settings need to know how well children are helped to learn and develop and how effectively children's welfare is promoted.*
>
> **Department for Education (2012)**

This key area of the inspection framework relates to the quality of the enabling, learning environment and the way that children are supported, included and motivated to learn. In addition, the ways in which the role of the adult/s contributes to this is important. Observing practice and provision, and reading records relating to Observation, Assessment and Planning during the visit will enable inspectors to make an accurate judgement about how well the provision enables children to learn and develop. In this way, it has strong links with the area of outcomes for children.

The quality of the provision comes about as a result of:

1. **A shared vision across the team being put into practice indoors and outdoors**
2. **Continuous provision being established, maintained and enhanced**
3. **Observation being used as a tool to develop provision in line with children's needs and interests**
4. **Daily, weekly, termly and annual planning systems that are used flexibly to support and include all children.**

The provision needs to support:

- **a secure foundation through learning and development opportunities that are planned around the needs and interests of each individual child, and are assessed and reviewed regularly**

- **the seven areas of learning and development:**

  - **Prime: Communication and Language, Physical, and Personal, Social and Emotional Development**

  - **Specific: Literacy, Mathematics, Knowledge of the World, and Expressive Arts and Design.**

(EYFS Statutory Guidance, Department for Education, 2012)

Inspectors will evaluate and make judgements about:

- **how well children are helped to learn and develop**
- **how effectively children's welfare is promoted**
- **how well adults support learning and development**
- **the quality of the learning environment indoors and outdoors**
- **the quality of planning**
- **how well information from observation and assessment is used and shared between staff and parents/carers.**

You and the team you work with will need to self-evaluate how well you provide for children through:

An accessible indoor environment

- **the quality of planning and how well observation and assessment indoors are used to plan the next steps for children**

- **creating a 'wow' factor indoors through:**

  - **the quality and range of easily accessible resources for children**

  - **appropriate storage: clean, bright and well maintained, including signs and notices**

  - **access to lots of natural materials**

- **appropriate balance of table top and floor-based activities**

- **how well the routine of the day works to meet children's needs.**

B An accessible outdoor environment

- the quality of planning and how well observation and assessment outdoors are used to plan the next steps for children
- creating a 'wow' factor outdoors through:
  - quality and a range of resources that are easily accessible to children
  - includes signs and notices: bigger, bolder, messier and noisier
  - appropriate storage
  - water supply via a tap and/or water butt
  - well maintained – natural not harsh
  - zoned areas
  - different surfaces
  - lots of natural materials, including things growing
- how well the routine of the day works to meet children's needs.

C The way adults support and facilitate learning and development

- use a range of interactive and other strategies to support children using the environment
- adding to the provision
- acting as a role model
- initiating activities and experiences
- demonstrating skills or sharing knowledge
- acknowledging and articulating a child's interests, actions or feelings, for example, running commentary or repeating back
- sharing own experiences in conversational style
- scaffolding learning for individual children
- asking questions and posing problems
- intervening when appropriate
- encouraging children, for example, to explore or investigate
- motivating and fostering interests.

D Effective planning

- long and medium term
- short term
    - including circle/group time
    - focused/adult-led activities
    - targeted activities.

E Effective assessment for learning

The process of assessment for learning is about taking evidence from several sources and analysing it to reveal what it tells us in respect of each child:

- **their needs**
- **their responses to what is on offer**
- **their current interests and achievements, as well as all other dimensions of their unique nature**
- **their stage/s of learning and development**
- **how well additional learning or development needs are met**
- **the next steps in their learning and development.**

F The extent to which there is planned, purposeful play and exploration indoors and outdoors – with an appropriate balance of adult-led and child-initiated, active learning fostered

- **steps taken by key persons to safeguard and protect children**
- **how good health and well-being are encouraged**
- **how well children are encouraged to develop the habits and behaviours of good learners**
- **the suitability and safety of outdoor and indoor spaces, furniture, equipment and toys.**

Chapter 4

Effective leadership and management

The effectiveness of leadership and management of the early years provision

The effectiveness of the setting's self-evaluation, including the steps taken to promote improvement. This judgement makes a significant contribution towards that for leadership and management, and for the setting's capacity for sustained improvement.

Ofsted Guidance for Inspectors (April 2012)

Within this key area of the framework, inspectors will seek to identify that there is adequate and effective ongoing support and advice for colleagues, including an induction programme for new staff. Self-evaluation procedures need to be securely in place and be reviewed and updated regularly so as to accurately assess the quality of education and care provided. This will be used to create a setting development plan, with all staff having appropriate opportunities to engage and participate in training based on the needs of the setting and those of individual staff. Clear procedures will need to be in place for effective and purposeful supervision of all staff as well as

an astute and targeted professional development programme for the whole staff team.

Ofsted (July 2012)

There should be regular time allocated for one-to-one meetings between management and individual staff, during which professional development needs and opportunities are discussed. Regular staff meetings should take place, where staff can contribute to the agenda and the items discussed, and regular and sufficient time should be given to staff teams to develop plans together.

Not only should the setting be checked for hazards at the start of each day, but risk assessments should be carried out on an ongoing basis to identify potential or existing dangers, including on the premises, equipment and activities, as well as trips out of the school/setting.

A clearly written and up-to-date health and safety policy needs to be in place and all practitioners should be aware of this. They should take up their responsibilities for health and safety under the guidance of a named person, who takes up the overall responsibility for this area. This includes clear awareness of policies and procedures for fire safety and fire drills, and checks of equipment taking place regularly, as well as first aid equipment being frequently maintained and monitored.

All practitioners should be aware of and receive a basic level of child protection training. It is important that they are supported by a suitably experienced child protection officer in the school/setting.

Management must ensure that the setting is well organised, including having additional adults available to allow for flexibility throughout the day, with all adults aware of emergency procedures regarding ratios.

Reflections/self-evaluations should focus on:

- **how effectively the key responsibilities of the EYFS lead/setting manager are implemented, including having a shared vision with the team on ways to move towards being outstanding**
- **the effectiveness of embedding an ambitious vision**
- **the quality, comprehensiveness and up-to-date nature of all records**
- **policies that reflect good practice in the setting**
- **the suitability and qualifications of practitioners, and the effectiveness of recruitment processes**
- **the quality and effectiveness of risk assessments**
- **effective and efficient use of available resources, including training for staff**
- **the effectiveness of links with parents and others to the integration of education and care**
- **the quality of the induction process for new staff.**

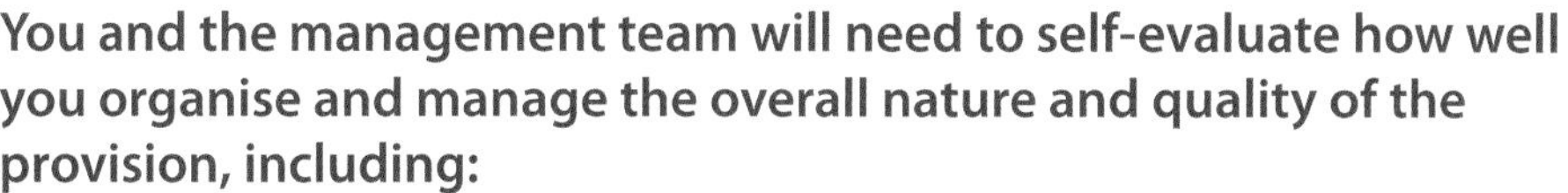
You and the management team will need to self-evaluate how well you organise and manage the overall nature and quality of the provision, including:

A How do you ensure staff training needs are met, and how do you then monitor and evaluate the effectiveness and impact of this on practice and outcomes for children?

- **Does training link to individual needs and the school/setting development plan?**
- **Is there a peer system of support, such as a buddy system, which ensures all staff can access support and advice from others in the team?**
- **Does appraisal take place in well organised and effective ways?**

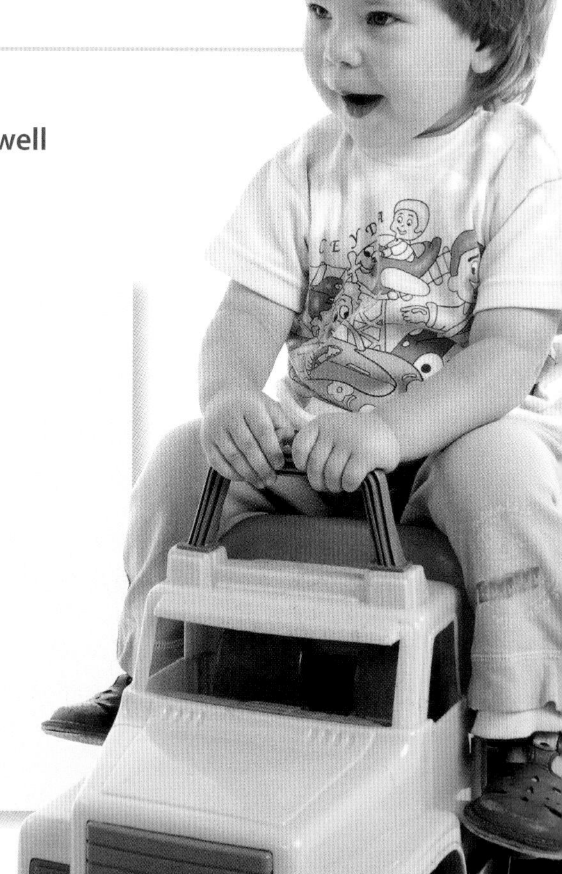

B How effective is the recruitment process from the application/interview stage, right through to induction and starting work at the school/setting?

- **Are the right people being recruited and retained?**
- **How is the application/interview stage managed effectively?**
- **Are CRB checks all in place and up to date?**
- **What is the staff turnover rate and are quality/experienced staff being retained?**

C How does management reflect on the importance of team meetings taking place?

- **These are planned on a weekly/regular basis and are prioritised to take place.**
- **Simple records of meetings are kept.**
- **Management attend on some occasions.**
- **Management are provided with records of meetings and respond as appropriate to these.**
- **All the team have input into the meeting agenda.**

How does management ensure that all written policies reflect both good practice and what all staff do consistently?

- **Policies are reviewed and updated by the staff team.**
- **Management monitor practice and feed back to staff.**
- **Parents, as well as staff, are involved in updating/reviewing policies.**
- **Named officers are in place and receive any necessary training on an ongoing basis.**
- **A setting development plan supports this.**

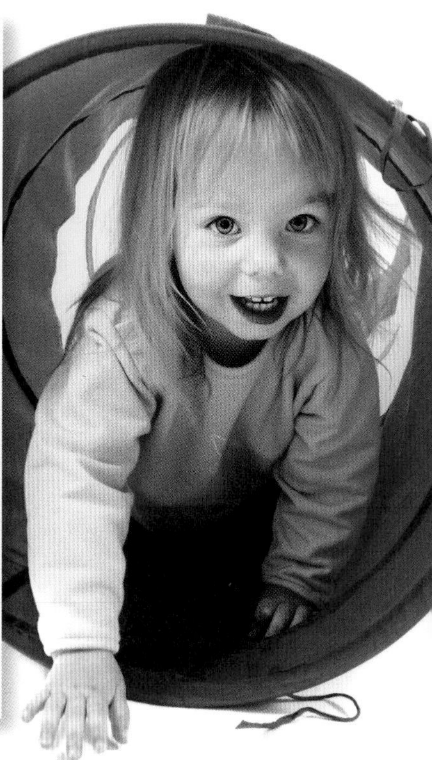

E How does management ensure that self-evaluation is effective, purposeful and leads to improved outcomes?

- **All staff are involved in the process.**
- **A structured and organised approach is used.**
- **Staff take their responsibilities, bringing up any issues with management that they feel need immediate attention.**
- **Management respond promptly and appropriately to any issues raised by staff.**
- **Regular observations are made on the provision and some outline notes made, including observations of staff working with children, and these are constructively fed back to individual staff and to the team as appropriate.**

F How does management ensure the provision is well organised and meets the needs of all children?

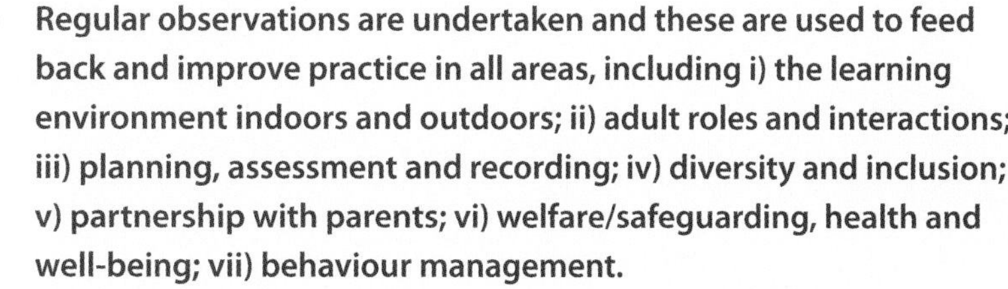

- **Regular observations are undertaken and these are used to feed back and improve practice in all areas, including i) the learning environment indoors and outdoors; ii) adult roles and interactions; iii) planning, assessment and recording; iv) diversity and inclusion; v) partnership with parents; vi) welfare/safeguarding, health and well-being; vii) behaviour management.**

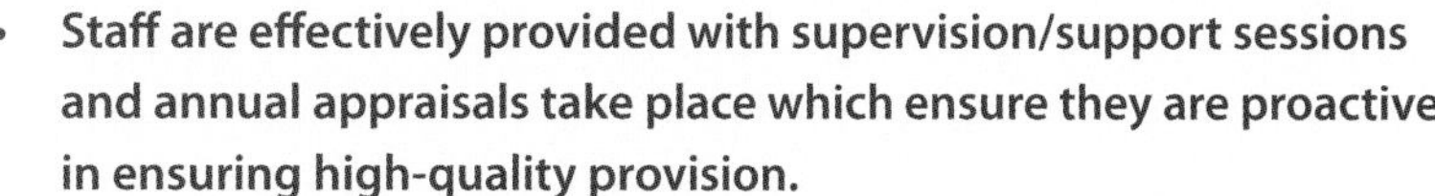

- **Staff are effectively provided with supervision/support sessions and annual appraisals take place which ensure they are proactive in ensuring high-quality provision.**

- **Staff are empowered to make simple changes in their rooms as these become necessary, or to take matters to management when issues begin to concern them which need a whole-team response.**
- **Self-evaluation is used as a strong and effective tool for monitoring and improvement within the setting.**
- **Parent/carer feedback is both actively sought and welcomed.**

The use of self-evaluation audits (see Chapter 6) as a whole team can be a particularly useful tool and is highly recommended, as this supports structured and organised focus and reflection on specific points and issues within this area.

Strong and effective leadership, management and organisation are key to a setting being outstanding. This underpins every element of what is provided for children and has strong links to the area of Overall Effectiveness within the inspection framework.

Chapter 5
Overall effectiveness

The overall quality and standards of the early years provision – one in which education and care are recognised as being inseparable

> "Children should have access to high-quality early years provision in order to make the most of their talents and abilities.
>
> **Ofsted (July 2012)**"

Overall effectiveness is about ensuring that each and every child's individual and group needs are both recognised and met. Practitioners in settings that achieve well in this aspect of the inspection framework really know their children and families well, and work closely in partnership with parents/carers and other professionals/agencies. This section looks at the bigger picture of what it is like for each and every child attending the provision and this includes children with special education needs, children with additional needs and children for whom English is an additional language. It covers how well settings identify and respond to children's individual interests, as well as their likes and dislikes. Evidence for this aspect can include both qualitative and quantitative types. A data file can be strong evidence that all children are achieving well based on their starting points, but it can also show evidence that this is not the case. This is why the analysis of the data and the setting's response to this is important to record and use.

Self-evaluating on overall effectiveness is about seeing improvements to the bigger picture and how these will impact on the complex nature of learning and teaching. Sometimes this will be on key aspects that are smaller parts but which affect things in big ways. Routines of the day can be one such smaller part that makes a big impact on how it is for all children.

In effective settings, practitioners recognise the importance of routines that are flexible enough to allow children to initiate their own learning, but are also structured in consistent ways to support children knowing what happens next. Settings that demonstrate strong overall effectiveness provide an inclusive environment for all the children: one in which the children are all happy, confident, emotionally strong and ready to learn.

> Aiming for provision that ensures all children are supported to make effective progress, especially those whose needs or circumstances require particularly perceptive intervention and/or additional support. In any particular provision, this may include:
>
> - **disabled children, as defined by the Equality Act 2010, and those who have special educational needs**
> - **boys**
> - **girls**
> - **groups of children with starting points that are significantly below those expected for their age**
> - **those who are easily able to exceed expectations for their age**
> - **children from disadvantaged families and/or backgrounds, including:**
>   - **funded two-year-olds***
>   - **looked after children**
>   - **children for whom English is an additional language**
>   - **children of service families**
>
> **Ofsted (July 2012)**
>
> * e.g in registered settings

This chapter will focus on:

- **welfare promotion**
- **effectiveness of self-evaluation**
- **trends in outcomes of progress**
- **the way needs are met of all children, including those with additional and special needs**
- **use of action plans.**

Principles into practice – collecting qualitative and quantitative data

When settings are inspected, more often than not, inspectors raise a number of areas that need to be addressed. These then become part of the starting points for the subsequent inspection when the inspection team will want to be assured that what was required has become appropriately embedded within practice and provision. In my experience, all settings do respond to this and make the advised improvements, but sometimes this is not embedded sufficiently and hence comes up again as a point for improvement. In such cases, this will become a limiting factor in judgements made.

Many settings not only undertake the improvements that are identified at the point of inspection, but many additional things too, based on the identified principles of good practice, as a result of their ongoing reflections, training and advice from consultants and others. What does not happen in enough cases is this being recorded in some form as added value. Hence, what is advised is that settings/schools set up an *Added Value File* which is used to gather together all the items that have been undertaken and provided since the last inspection, the reasons for these and the impact that these have had on outcomes for children.

The heading within the file should be led by the actions they depict, for example, some around smaller grouping, key person role could come under a heading of Adult Role, whilst those around indoor and outdoor play might come under Enabling Environments, and those around planning under the heading of Observation, Assessment and Planning, and so on. The evidence can be varied and include images (before and after), written supporting explanations, new formats and children's work, for example, samples of writing.

Where good practice audits are completed, these can be placed in the file along with the actions that these identified.

The *Added Value File* helps to support a wider understanding of the vision of the setting, and reflects the large amount of work that practitioners undertake for the benefit of the children. As well as providing supporting evidence for the Ofsted judgement under leadership and management namely that:

> "the pursuit of excellence in all the setting's activities is demonstrated by an uncompromising highly successful as well as documented drive to strongly improve achievement and maintain the highest levels of achievement for all children over a sustained period of time.
>
> **Ofsted (July 2012)**"

What we do is not primarily for the purposes of Ofsted, but for the children, so that they get the best start in their life but we would be naive in this age of accountability to ignore the importance of gaining recognition for what we do through an Ofsted inspection and the fact that the report will be published and made available for the general public, including our parent/s and carers, to read. We therefore would want it to give a true reflection of our provision and practice. An *Added Value File* is supportive of this as it provides evidence that demonstrates improvement to our provision in qualitative ways. Ofsted of course will also be looking at the data on children's achievements and rates of progress alongside this, which is the quantitative aspect. Hence, it is also advised that settings set up a *data file* that should include:

- **group/class lists with the date of entry – this can be in key person grouping but does not have to be**
- **current/up-to-date years' data, which, subject to the stage/age of the child, will relate to Development Matters or ELGs, which should be updated at least three times a year**
- **the past three years' data of children in the group/class to give a trend (in a school reception class this will be the EYFS profile)**
- **analysis of significant groupings within the data, for example, by gender, by ethnicity, by free school meals (if in EYFS school provision) and notes of action planned/taken to support underachievement.**

You will find that this is a very useful tool for self-evaluation purposes and something that is also extremely useful as evidence when Ofsted inspect. It not only provides evidence of outcomes for children, but also supports evidence of effective management and organisation.

Chapter 6
Good practice audits

Watch over us. Wrap us up against the cold and rain, and give us shade from the hot sun. Make sure we have enough to eat and drink, and if we are sick, nurse and comfort us.

United Nations Convention on the Rights of the Child (2000)

The revised EYFS Framework guidance (Department for Education, 2012) has a strong emphasis on reflection and self-evaluation among Early Years teams and individual practitioners. The following two good practice audits have been produced to enable teams to begin to focus on where they consider the best starting points are for them. Learning and Development and Inclusion are the two audits provided and can be completed just in the parts required or in their entirety. It will be up to individual teams in settings to make that decision.

The two audits are provided for practicioners to use as an approach to good practice from two different perspectives. Although they are designed to be filled in, they can also be used as a tool for talking about current practice and possible future improvements. Actions decided can then be added to the setting's development plans.

The audits should be used, among other things, to:

- **celebrate existing good practice**
- **identify growth areas for improvement**
- **identify and arrange staff training needs**
- **support effective and strong leadership, management and organisation within the setting**
- **ensure that outcomes for all children become consistently good or better.**

The two audits are:

1. **Learning and Development Audit**
2. **Inclusion Audit.**

Learning and Development Audit

Linked to the Four Themes of the Revised EYFS

PRIME AREA of Communication and Language	Audit notes	Rating 1– 4
Positive relationships		
Help children to communicate thoughts, ideas and feelings, and build up relationships.		
Give daily opportunities to share and enjoy a wide range of music, songs and poetry.		
Model language for children e.g. using commentary techniques.		
Identify and respond to any particular difficulties in children's language development at an early stage.		
Enabling environments		
Provide time and relaxed opportunities for children to develop spoken language through sustained conversations between children and adults, both one-to-one and in small groups, and between the children themselves.		
Allow children time to initiate conversations, respect their thinking time and silences, and help them to develop the interaction skills.		
Show particular awareness of, and sensitivity to, the needs of children learning English as an additional language, using their home language when appropriate and ensuring close teamwork between practitioners, parents and bilingual workers, so that the children's developing use of English and other languages support each other.		
Provide an environment that stimulates children and, through cosy spaces, that encourages them to communicate.		

PRIME AREA of Communication and Language (contd.)	Audit notes	Rating 1– 4
Learning and development		
Link language with physical movement in action songs and rhymes, role play and practical experiences, such as cookery and gardening.		
Show sensitivity to the many different ways that children express themselves both verbally and non-verbally and encourage children to communicate their thoughts, ideas and feelings through a range of expressive forms, such as body movement, art, dance and songs.		
Talk to children and engage them as partners in conversation.		
Develop children's phonological awareness, particularly through rhyme and alliteration, and their knowledge of the alphabetic code.		
Unique child		
Talk with children about their experiences, both in the setting and at home.		
Observe children and use this to provide for individual children's learning needs by considering each child's stage of development and the next steps for them.		
Encourage and respond positively to individual children's communications.		

PRIME AREA of Physical Development	Audit notes	Rating 1–4
Positive relationships		
Build children's confidence to take manageable risks in their play.		
Motivate children to be active and help them to develop movement skills through praise, encouragement, games and appropriate guidance.		
Notice and value children's natural and spontaneous movements, through which they are finding out about their bodies and exploring sensations such as balance.		
Provide time to support children's understanding of how exercise, eating, sleeping and hygiene promote good health.		
Enabling environments		
Provide equipment and resources that are sufficient, challenging and interesting, and that can be used in a variety of ways, or to support specific physical skills.		
Allow sufficient time and opportunities for children with physical disabilities or motor impairments to develop their physical skills, working in partnership with relevant specialists, such as physiotherapists and occupational therapists.		
Use additional adult help as necessary to support individuals and to encourage increased independence in physical activities.		

PRIME AREA of Physical Development (contd.)	Audit notes	Rating 1–4
Learning and development		
Plan activities that offer physical challenges and plenty of opportunities for physical activity.		
Give sufficient time for children to use a range of equipment to persist in activities, practising new and existing skills, and learning from their mistakes.		
Introduce appropriate vocabulary to children alongside their actions.		
Treat mealtimes as an opportunity to promote children's social development, while enjoying food and highlighting the importance of making healthy choices.		
Unique child		
Support individual children who are less confident or skillful in using small tools and equipment, or large equipment.		
Observe how children use resources, tools and equipment and, where appropriate, use this to provide appropriately targeted or extended opportunities e.g. next steps.		
Follow individual children's natural interests by providing enhancements to existing provision to support individual physical skills.		

PRIME AREA of Personal, Social and Emotional Development	Audit notes	Rating 1–4
Positive relationships		
Form warm, caring attachments with children in the group.		
Establish constructive relationships with parents, everyone in the setting and workers from other agencies.		
Take opportunities to give encouragement to children, with practitioners acting as role models who value differences and take account of different needs and expectations.		
Plan for opportunities for children to play and learn, sometimes alone and sometimes in groups of varying sizes in child-initiated and adult-led activities.		
Enabling environments		
Ensure that each child has a key person and knows who that person is.		
Ensure sufficient time and space are provided for children to concentrate on activities and experiences, and to develop their own interests.		
Provide a range of positive images that challenge children's thinking and help them to embrace differences in gender, ethnicity, language, religion and culture, special educational needs and disabilities.		
Establish opportunities for play and learning that acknowledge children's particular religious beliefs and cultural backgrounds.		
Support the development of independence skills, particularly for children who are highly dependent upon adult support for personal care.		

PRIME AREA of Personal, Social and Emotional Development (contd.)	Audit notes	Rating 1–4
Learning and development		
Plan activities that promote emotional, moral, spiritual and social development, together with intellectual development.		
Provide experiences that help children to develop autonomy and a disposition to learn.		
Give support and a structured approach to learning for vulnerable children and those with particular behavioural or communication difficulties, to help them achieve successful Personal, Social and Emotional Development.		
Unique child		
Support children to make individual, meaningful and appropriate choices.		
Consider each child's stage of development and use this to support their learning and development appropriately.		
Support children exploring their individual likes, dislikes and associated preferences.		
Use ongoing observations of individual children to provide sensitive support and recognition of individual and differing needs within the group.		
Follow and support individual children's interests and needs.		

SPECIFIC AREA of Literacy	Audit notes	Rating 1 – 4
Positive relationships		
Give daily opportunities to share and enjoy a wide range of fiction and non-fiction books, rhymes, music, songs, poetry and stories.		
Model reading and writing, and encourage children to experiment writing for themselves through making marks, personal writing symbols and conventional script.		
Identify and respond to children's literacy development by observing them in activities and then using this to provide the next steps from them.		
Accommodate children's specific religious or cultural beliefs.		
Enabling environments		
Plan an environment that is rich in signs, symbols, notices, numbers, words, rhymes, books, pictures, music and songs that take into account children's different interests, understandings, home backgrounds and cultures.		
As children develop, provide a range of independent reading opportunities within the learning environment.		
As children develop, provide a range of independent writing opportunities within the learning environment.		
Provide appropriate books in the developed/defined spaces relating to the resources in these.		
Provide simple props so children can play out the characters and actions of familiar stories both indoors and outdoors.		

SPECIFIC AREA of Literacy (contd.)	Audit notes	Rating 1–4
Learning and development		
For children who may need to use alternative communication systems, provide opportunities for them to discover ways of recording ideas and to gain access to texts in an alternative way, for example, through ICT.		
Show children that what they say can be written and read.		
Make whole-class books to help and support engagement with children's literacy skills.		
Provide a range of stimulating and exciting mark-making tools and resources, such as writing to go boxes, writing sacks and writing belts, jumbo chalk, glitter pens etc.		
Unique child		
Support, encourage and create opportunities for children to express their ideas in a range of ways, including drawing and writing, and respond to these.		
Support individual children to access the literate environment, particularly those who appear less confident.		

SPECIFIC AREA of Maths	Audit notes	Rating 1– 4
Positive relationships		
Give children sufficient time, space and encouragement to discover and use new words, and mathematical ideas, concepts and language during child-initiated play and other activities.		
Encourage children to explore real-life problems, to make patterns, and to count and match together, for example, ask 'How many spoons do we need for everyone in the group to have one?'		
Support children who use a means of communication other than spoken English to develop and understand specific mathematical language, while valuing knowledge of mathematics in the language or communication system they use at home.		
Value children's graphic and practical explorations of mathematical ideas.		
Enabling environments		
Recognise the mathematical potential of the outdoor environment, for example, for children to discover things about shape, distance and measures through their physical activity.		
Exploit the mathematical potential of the indoor environment, for example, enabling children to discover things about numbers, counting and calculating through practical activities, such as finding out how many children are in the music area or how many books a child has looked at today.		
Ensure a wide range of mathematical resources are readily available both indoors and outside.		

SPECIFIC AREA of Maths (contd.)	Audit notes	Rating 1– 4
Learning and development		
Develop mathematical understanding through all children's early experiences, including stories, songs, games and imaginative play.		
Provide a range of activities, some of which focus on mathematical learning and some which enable mathematical learning to be drawn out, for example, exploring shape, size and pattern during block play.		
Model the mathematical language during play and daily routines.		
Unique child		
Show interest in individual children's play and mathematical learning and development, offering encouragement and challenge through open-ended questioning, such as 'How many will…?' and 'What would happen if…?' to support problem solving and other skills.		
Observe children and use this to plan and provide for individual mathematical learning needs e.g. next steps and enhancements to extend individual children's play.		
Encourage individual children's exploration of materials and their properties e.g. size, shape and texture.		

SPECIFIC AREA of Understanding of the World	Audit notes	Rating 1–4
Positive relationships		
Use parents' knowledge to extend children's experience of the world.		
Help children to become aware of, explore and question difference in gender, ethnicity, language, religion, culture, special educational needs and disability issues.		
Support children with sensory impairment by providing supplementary experience and information to enhance their learning about the world around them.		
Enabling environments		
Create a stimulating environment that offers a range of activities that will encourage children's interest and curiosity, both indoors and outdoors.		
Make effective use of outdoors, including the local neighbourhood.		
Use correct terms so that, for example, children will enjoy naming a chrysalis if the practitioner uses the correct name.		
Pose carefully framed open-ended questions, such as 'How can we…?' or 'What would happen if…?'.		

SPECIFIC AREA of Understanding of the World (contd.)	Audit notes	Rating 1– 4
Learning and development		
Plan activities based on first-hand experiences that encourage exploration, experimentation, observation, problem solving, prediction, critical thinking, decision making and discussion.		
Teach skills and knowledge in the context of practical activities, for example, learning about the characteristics of liquids and solids by involving children in melting chocolate or cooking eggs.		
Encourage children to tell each other what they have found out, to speculate on future findings or to describe their experiences. This enables them to rehearse and reflect upon their knowledge and to practise new vocabulary.		
Support children in using ICT to include cameras, photocopiers, CD players, tape recorders and programmable toys, in addition to computers.		
Give children accurate information that challenges cultural, racial, social and gender stereotypes.		
Unique child		
Observe and find out which resources, equipment and materials are particularly stimulating and interesting to individuals and groups of children, and use this to purposefully enhance and develop the daily provision.		
Encourage, listen carefully and positively respond to individual children's actions and communications about their learning.		
Through observations, consider the children's stage of development so as to support their needs and interests appropriately to ensure all children make appropriately good progress.		

SPECIFIC AREA of Expressive Arts and Design	Audit notes	Rating 1– 4
Positive relationships		
Ensure children feel secure enough to have a go, learn new things and be adventurous.		
Value what children can do and children's own ideas rather than expecting them to reproduce someone else's picture, dance or model (for example).		
Give opportunities for children to work alongside artists and other creative adults so that they see at first hand different ways of expressing and communicating ideas, and different responses to media and materials.		
Accommodate children's specific religious or cultural beliefs relating to particular forms of art or methods of representation.		
Enabling environments		
Provide a stimulating environment in which creativity, originality and expressiveness are valued.		
Include resources from a variety of cultures to stimulate new ideas and different ways of thinking.		
Offer opportunities for children with hearing impairment to experience sound through physical contact with artefacts, materials, spaces and movements.		
Encourage children who cannot communicate by voice to respond to music in different ways, such as gestures.		

SPECIFIC AREA of Expressive Arts and Design (contd.)	Audit notes	Rating 1–4
Learning and development		
Present a wide range of experiences and activities that children can respond to by using many of their senses.		
Allow sufficient time for children to explore and develop ideas, and finish working through these ideas.		
Create opportunities for children to express their ideas through a wide range of types of representation.		
Unique child		
Follow and support individual children's ideas and interests by appropriately making tools and resources accessible, and enhancing with additional resources as necessary.		
Allow children sufficient time and space to use their own ideas to explore and create.		
Support children's individual curiosity through open-ended questions, such as 'What would happen if…?'.		
Through observations, consider children's stage of development so as to support their needs and interests appropriately to ensure all children make appropriately good progress.		

Inclusion audit for EYFS settings

This inclusion audit is broken down into six sections, each with a range of indicators:

1. **Environmental**
2. **Leadership and Management**
3. **The Team**
4. **Child's Voice**
5. **Parents'/carers' Voice**
6. **Policies and Paperwork**

Using this audit, you will be able to celebrate the things you do well and prioritise any action/planning for improvements you may need to put into place. Position statements and judgements based on the four descriptors for each of the key sections are as follows:

1. **Focusing – includes some of the minimum requirements but needs improvement.**
2. **Developing – includes a high proportion of the minimum requirements.**
3. **Enabling – progress above the minimum requirements has become embedded into daily practice.**
4. **Enhancing – a consistent, high quality, creative approach to practice has been established.**

NB Where judgements are between these, it is possible to make a rating judgment reflecting this, for example, ½ or ¾.

Practitioners should use one section at a time for self-evaluation through whole-team discussions. From these discussions, a position statement should then be created and a grade given on each of the indicators using the scale 1–4:

1. **Focusing (inadequate)**
2. **Developing (satisfactory)**
3. **Enabling (good)**
4. **Enhancing (outstanding).**

NB It is possible to grade as ½ or ¾ where this is appropriate/helpfully accurate.

Inclusion audit

Environmental What visitors to the setting will see consistently going on all the time	Position statements	Rating 1– 4
Children with disabilities are included appropriately. This practice is seen as the 'norm' and the ethos demonstrated through positive attitudes and behaviours of all practitioners and children in the setting.		
The setting is well prepared to include children with disabilities through existing policy, practice and provision.		
Practitioners are very responsive to children's needs and interests. They think on their feet and ensure they readily provide themselves as a resource.		
The needs, interests and enthusiasm of each of the children who attend are used to lead the planning or provision of activities that take place, sensitively taking into account any likes and dislikes, and specific needs of each child.		
Each child's individual background and characteristics are taken fully into account.		
Each and every child is welcomed on arrival and wished well on leaving in a way that suits them.		

Environmental (contd.) **What visitors to the setting will see consistently going on all the time**	**Position statements**	**Rating 1– 4**
Equipment and resources, including displays and images in and around the setting, appropriately reflect disabled people's lives and a range of different cultures.		
All cases of discriminatory language and behaviour are addressed and discussed sensitively with any adults or children involved. These cases and actions taken are recorded appropriately.		
Children and adults freely initiate communication with one another about interests, needs and progress, and important related issues. The key person role is reflected strongly within this communication.		
Each child is able to choose to play alongside others, play with others or not to play with others. Practitioners sensitively address the issues if any child is consistently being excluded from others' play.		
Each child and adult is respected and valued as an individual with equal rights and choices, and given the chance to exercise those rights.		
Assessed acceptable risk is available to each child to ensure both safety and excitement through a carefully planned and developed enabling environment, both indoors and outdoors.		

Leadership and Management **What actions have already taken place and how committed are leaders and managers to things being in place in the future?**	**Position statements**	**Rating 1–4**
There is a commitment from leaders and managers to the active participation of children, parents/carers, team members and others in processes that ensure good quality provision, where all individual needs are met.		
Leaders and managers are able to identify actions taken and progress already made towards inclusion and current priorities. The development plans of the setting, and the things the setting still needs to do to be more inclusive.		
Leaders and managers have made, and continue to make, all reasonable adjustments for better physical access to, and around, the setting.		
Leaders and managers hold regular team meetings to reflect on practice together as a team and to develop future good practice.		
Leaders and managers have deployed and continue to deploy sources of funding where necessary to support the inclusion of children.		
Leaders and managers have effectively built links with local disabled people who can contribute effectively as part of a wide cross-section of adults involved in the work of the setting.		
Leaders and managers access appropriate support and advice from colleagues and other expert professionals.		

The Team Training, attitudes and skills	Position statements	Rating 1–4
The whole team have had attitudinal training around disability and other equality issues, and continue to take part in training on inclusion on a regular basis.		
The early attendance at attitudinal training is part of the induction process for all new staff.		
All the team are aware that attitudes, environments, structures, policies and practice need regular review/updating in order that no child is disadvantaged.		
All staff feel that they are well informed and consulted by managers/leaders.		
Each member of the team has or is developing the necessary skills to communicate effectively with each child and to encourage all children to develop ways of communicating with one another.		
Each member of staff is able to describe the systems in place to respond to any individual child who may need specific assistance.		
All staff know and use children's and adults' chosen/preferred names.		
All staff use consistent, positive language and are confident about explaining why that terminology is preferred and used.		
All staff create opportunities to communicate with each child and their parents/carers to discuss how best to build on children's interests, meet their needs and promote their participation.		

Child's Voice Individual children	Position statements	Rating 1–4
Each child has the opportunity for both formal and informal conferencing/consultation with their key person or preferred other adults. This is done using whatever communication methods they choose.		
Each child feeds back when asked and practitioners actively seek their views and pay attention to their requests.		
Each child indicates that they are generally happy in the setting.		
Each child is helped to show their parent/carer what they have been doing. This includes those children who have difficulty with communication.		
Parents'/carers' Voice **Parents'/carers'**	**Position statements**	**Rating 1–4**
Each parent/carer feels welcomed and valued as an expert on their child, with a continuing key role in helping practitioners (including their child's key person) to enable their child to feel safe and involved.		
Each parent/carer is provided with a variety of opportunities for formal and informal consultation about provision and practice within the setting, and feels able to influence what is going on in the setting as a whole, and is comfortable approaching practitioners to discuss issues.		
Each parent/carer feels there is a settled and happy atmosphere in the setting and is content with the experiences and opportunities available to their children.		

Policies and paperwork Indicate/reflect permeation of ethos and commitment	Position statements	Rating 1–4
A commitment exists to meet individual children's needs and creating an inclusive ethos.		
The setting states and demonstrates that it will do all it can to make every child equally welcome.		
Practitioners who have a specific role in assisting one particular disabled child are clear that their responsibilities focus on the inclusion of the child, as well as whatever level of individual assistance may be necessary. These workers are seen as full and equal members of the team and valued as such.		
Written information about each child includes details of how best to meet their needs, procedures for any care or medical requirements, and a risk assessment/personal plan where appropriate.		
The setting's vision, policies and procedures are clearly documented and a process of monitoring and self-evaluation to see how well it is doing is in place. This includes all who are involved in the setting in a process of continuing reflection on the development of inclusive policy and practice.		

Bibliography and further reading

DfE (April 2012) *Guidance for Inspectors of EYFS Provision* Crown Publication

DfE (July 2012) *Evaluation Schedule for Inspections of Registered Early Years Providers* Crown Publication

DfE (2012) *The Statutory Framework for the Early Years Foundation Stage*

Keller and Price (2011) *Beyond Performance* John Wiley & Sons

Early Education (2012) *Development Matters in the EYFS*

DfES (2004) *Every Child Matters* DfES

Gould, T. (2011) *Effective Practice in Outdoor Learning* Featherstone

Gould, T., Brierley, J., and Coates-Mohammed, K. (2012) *Learning and Playing Indoors* Featherstone

Gould, T. (2012) *Effective Transition in the Early Years* Featherstone

Abbott, L. and Nutbrown, C. (2001) *Experiencing Reggio Emilia* OU Press

Featherstone, S. and Bayley, R. (2001) *Foundations for Independence* Featherstone